DANCING TO DESTINY

My Dance Journey to the Anointing and
Praise Dance Ministry Manual

ANDREA GUILLORY

DANCING TO DESTINY

Copyright © 2020 Andrea Guillory

All rights reserved. Printed in the United States of America. No part of this book may be used or reproduced in any manner whatsoever without written permission except in the case of brief quotations in critical articles or reviews.

Cover Design, Typesetting, Book Layout by
Enger Lanier Taylor for In Due Season Publishing

Published By: In Due Season Publishing
                    Huntsville, Alabama
                    indueseasonpublishing@gmail.com
                    www.indueseasonpublishing.com

ISBN-13: 978-1-970057-07-2
ISBN-10: 1-970057-07-6

www.andreaguillory.com
Facebook Search: @danceforyourfreedom
Instagram: @_AndreaGuillory_ /Twitter: @AndreaGuillor16
Periscope: @_AndreaGuillory_
Email: info@andreaguillory.com

Scripture quotations marked (NIV) are taken from the Holy Bible, New International Version®, NIV®. Copyright © 1973, 1978, 1984, 2011 by Biblica, Inc.® Used by permission of Zondervan. All rights reserved worldwide. www.zondervan.com The "NIV" and "New International Version" are trademarks registered in the United States Patent and Trademark Office by Biblica, Inc.®

Scripture taken from the New King James Version®. Copyright © 1982 by Thomas Nelson. Used by permission. All rights reserved.

The ESV® Bible (The Holy Bible, English Standard Version®) is adapted from the Revised Standard Version of the Bible, copyright Division of Christian Education of the National Council of the Churches of Christ in the U.S.A. All rights reserved.

Scripture quotations marked MSG are taken from THE MESSAGE, copyright © 1993, 2002, 2018 by Eugene H. Peterson. Used by permission of NavPress. All rights reserved. Represented by Tyndale House Publishers, a Division of Tyndale House Ministries.

Scripture quotations are taken from the Holy Bible, New Living Translation, copyright ©1996, 2004, 2015 by Tyndale House Foundation. Used by permission of Tyndale House Publishers, a Division of Tyndale House Ministries, Carol Stream, Illinois 60188. All rights reserved.

Scriptures marked KJV are taken from the King James Version (KJV): King James Version, public domain

CONTENTS

Dedications ....

Introduction 2

Chapter 1 3

Chapter 2 16

Chapter 3 24

Chapter 4 29

Chapter 5 36

Chapter 6 41

Chapter 7 46

Chapter 8 51

DEDICATIONS

I dedicate this book to my Lord and Savior, Jesus Christ. I am alive today because He kept me in my darkest hours and renewed my life. I'm thankful to my Mother, Lena Ledet, who nurtured me as a single Mom. Your life of serving the Lord and others gave me a servants heart.

To those who became my support on this journey, words cannot express my gratitude. Nathaniel and Donna Richardson, Paul and Kim Todd, Julian, and Brenda Guillory, may God bless you and keep you in His favor.

Next, I want to thank my mentor Michelle J. Miller-Boston, for pushing me to finish this book and into my Destiny. Thank you for equipping me with wisdom, knowledge, and the Word.

Lastly, I'm thankful to my children Taylor, Logan, and Lauren. You gave me strength through it all and believed God was going to work everything out for our good.

INTRODUCTION

Years ago, I sat in church and felt the Holy Spirit come over me through the praise dance ministers. I remember thinking to myself, "I can dance for the Lord." After all, I was a cheerleader throughout high school and college. We danced all the time. I didn't realize the giftings that were placed in me before my birth. I had natural energy, excitement, skill, and strength for movement. On my journey in the praise dance ministry, the Lord groomed me. I was taught ballet technique, the Word, how to seek a personal relationship with the Lord, and how to pray.

Who would have thought the praise dance ministry was not only about dancing? I was drawn to dance ministry for growth, healing, prayer, and deliverance; through it all, God gets the Glory! I was excited and on fire for God, so I decided to make Him Lord over my life. I remember hearing the choir singing, *"Lord Prepare Me To Be a Sanctuary."* Something in me desired to be a *sanctuary* for God. I wanted Holiness and more of His presence. Through all of my desires, the Lord used the praise dance ministry to ignite a fiery passion within me.

1

A CHOSEN PEOPLE

In Him we were also chosen, having been predestined according to the plan of him who works out everything in conformity with the purpose of his will.

Ephesians 1:11 (NIV)

After years of serving in the praise dance ministry, the Lord transitioned me to another church. During my time of transition, I thought my participation in the ministry of praise dance was over. I was thinking to myself, "I'll just sit on the pew for a minute, and I won't tell anyone that I am a dance minister." God had other plans. He gave someone the same dream I had and exposed the gift of dance we had in common. God is a comedian, and the joke was on me. This particular ministry was a church plant for the United Methodist Church. So, my sister in

Christ, and I developed the mission statement and the foundation for the praise dance ministry. We began to minister through dance, grow, and assist with building the church. I was astonished to know God would choose someone like me to help build a church. In a previous experience, I felt as though I wasn't worthy or holy enough at times. I felt as if I was the least of these, an outcast. The one who didn't fit in with the click and could no longer deal with being burnt out. Why would God choose me? I didn't have the skills to lead in praise dance. I was broken and felt rejected. Yet, I'm confident that the rejection that I experienced was so that God would be glorified. My past, sufferings, and failures of never feeling that I could get it right didn't change God's decision about my destiny. Our God looked beyond my shortcomings and saw my heart.

But the Lord said to Samuel, "Do not consider his appearance or his height, for I have rejected him. The Lord does not look at the things people look at. People look at the outward appearance, but the Lord looks at the heart."
1 Samuel 16:7 (NIV)

God is full of surprises. As I think about the story of David and the fact that his very own father didn't think enough of him to be considered as the one God had chosen. David was ostracized and rejected, so how could he be a chosen shepherd? I, too, was rejected and abandoned by my father. With the help of the Lord, I was able to forgive and heal in time. Realizing I had a heavenly Father who has been with me, leading and guiding me with His love.

*Jesse had seven of his sons pass before Samuel, but Samuel said to him, "The L*ORD *has not chosen these." ¹¹ So he asked Jesse, "Are these all the sons you have?" "There is still the youngest," Jesse answered. "He is tending the sheep." Samuel said, "Send for him; we will not sit down until he arrives." ¹² So he sent for him and had him brought in. He was glowing with health and had a fine appearance and handsome features. Then the L*ORD *said, "Rise and anoint him; this is the one." ¹³ So Samuel took the horn of oil and anointed him in the presence of his brothers, and from that day on the Spirit of the L*ORD *came powerfully upon David.* **1 Samuel 16:10-13 (NIV)**

As the Lord guided, I listened and began to press into the vision; I was excited. Well, at first, I was excited until I realized there was an extensive process to prepare for this thing called destiny. Like Joseph, I was excited and wanted to share the vision God gave to me with loved ones and those who played a vital part in this journey of dance. Unfortunately, I was laughed at or looked at strangely as though it was a joke. I was crushed and disappointed. Listen, when God gives you a dream, most will not understand. Joseph told his brothers about his dream. Consequently, they plotted to kill him and sold him into slavery.

When Joseph's brothers saw him coming, they recognized him in the distance. As he approached, they made plans to kill him. ¹⁹ "Here comes the dreamer!" they said. ²⁰ "Come on, let's kill him and throw him into one of these cisterns. We can tell our father, 'A wild animal has eaten him.' Then we'll see what becomes of his dreams!" **Genesis 37:18-28 (NLT)**

Judah said to his brothers, "What will we gain by killing our brother? We'd have to cover up the crime.[c] ²⁷ Instead of hurting him, let's sell him to those Ishmaelite traders. After all, he is our brother—our own flesh and blood!" And his brothers agreed. **Genesis 37:26 (NLT)**

King David, Joseph, and Jesus were all rejected! You will experience rejection on your way to destiny. Some will be jealous, mock, discourage, or think that you are crazy. However, you can't worry about the haters and dream killers. Your focus is obedience by any means necessary! I am convinced that the God we serve allowed the evil intensions to set Joseph up for his process so that he could be ready for the vision. The "process" is before the promise and the platform. So, forget about the past, what people think, and your imperfections. God can choose you! He's looking at your heart and looking for your "Yes."

By Grace

A few years later, in 2009, I woke up and heard the Lord whisper in my ear, "ANOINTED TO DANCE." He said He was calling me to the nations. Huh? I was excited but perplexed. I've never had dance training, and I can't create. The mere thought was too much and seemed impossible to me. All I could think about was how unqualified I was for such a huge task.

A hint to know that you are in the will of God is that it would be IMPOSSIBLE to do it without Him. God doesn't choose you based upon your qualifications but anoints you with His power and gives grace to fulfill His purpose. The Lord gave me the grace I needed to hear, move, and create through dance. It's always an out of body experience because I know my human abilities cannot comprehend the anointing on my life. It's only by His Grace. You don't need years of experience in dance, perfect dance technique, a degree in dance, or to become ordained by your church. The King of Glory isn't looking at the human perspective. It's a Godly perspective.

We have different gifts, according to the grace given to each of us. If your gift is prophesying, then prophesy in accordance with your faith. **Romans 12:6 (NIV)**

Zeal

When you are destined to succeed in an area or task, you must have passion and zeal. There's something inside of you that you can't let go. I remember joining the praise dance ministry for the first time. I was so excited to start this new journey, and I experienced the presence of God at every rehearsal. The anointing was so strong on our leader. The Lord used her to tap into the heavens so that we saw God break chains and show His miraculous power when worshipped and prayed. Of course, we practiced dance and prepared for messages to go forth. But this wasn't just a rehearsal. It was a time of intimacy, worship, prayer, prophecy, healing, encouragement, friendship, learning, and receiving. This ministry of dance belonged to God, and He marked and anointed it as His own. The anointing destroys the yokes and where the Spirit of the Lord is there is freedom.

When you believed, you were marked in him with a seal, the promised Holy Spirit, who is a deposit guaranteeing our inheritance until the redemption of those who are God's possession—to the praise of his glory. **Ephesians 1:13-14 (NIV)**

It shall come to pass in that day That his burden will be taken away from your shoulder, And his yoke from your neck, And the yoke will be destroyed because of the anointing oil. **Isaiah 10:27 (NKJV)**

Now the Lord is the Spirit, and where the Spirit of the Lord is, there is freedom. **2 Corinthians 3:17 (NIV)**

I came to an understanding of the authority of Jesus and the blood of the Lamb. God, Himself, came and delivered! The consistency of being in His presence and seeing His demonstrations gave me the zeal to run and never look back. I made a conscious decision to be "souled out" to Christ. When you're souled out, you have a made-up mind to serve God as your Lord and Savior. It means you pray about everything and let God take the lead and provide the necessary answers. I no longer make choices based on my own desires because I want to please God. I was so committed to the praise dance ministry that in three years, I never missed a rehearsal. I scheduled my life around rehearsals; that's zeal!

God developed me as an intercessor and a prayer warrior. During this time, I received the gift of tongues and began to walk in the office of a prophet

Never be lacking in zeal, but keep your spiritual fervor, serving the Lord. **Romans 12:11 (NIV)**

Who gave himself for us, that he might redeem us from all iniquity, and purify unto himself a peculiar people, zealous of good works. **Titus 2:14 (KJV)**

DANCING TO DESTINY

Merriam-Webster defines zeal as eagerness and ardent interest in the pursuit of something. Your zeal gives purpose to who you are and why you exist. You can hear the music, see the vision, and move to the beat. Even when you attempt to turn away from the task, yet something still pulls on you to look back and fulfill the mission. Despite your reservations, challenges, and obstacles along the course, you should always be committed to seeing it through. This desire and your "Yes" may cost you something, but it is nothing to be compared to the Glory that shall be revealed (Romans 8:18).

Intimacy with God

Intimacy with God is a direct impact for your public appearance. You can look at your intimate time with God as practice for the big game. In order to perform at your best, you must practice. Champions become winners because they go through extensive training to be the best. It's not because they are only gifted.

Practice. Practice. Practice. During this time, you can build your strength and strategy to master the game, study plays, and become familiar with your opponent's so you are better prepared to win. If you are not prepared for the game, you may miss plays, lose stamina, get hurt, and be confused about your position. As you get to know God, our Coach, He leads, protects, gives you understanding, and a plan to win. You get to know who He is, how He conditions, and how He creates divine strategies. The longer you are with the Coach who has a winning team, the more you can identify His ways, His Vision, and His voice. In His presence is where downloads are dropped, revelations are revealed, and peace (Shalom) is restored. You can be confident that He is going to lead you to victory. After all, His record is undefeated. You will learn that it is not just your position that carries the weight of the game, but it's a team effort. Michael Jordan says, "A great player can win a game, but it takes a team to win a championship."

Every team has a practice field and a set schedule to meet. Build an altar and let the presence of God dwell in the midst. Create a place and a time when you will meet the King. Specifically, I light candles, lay pillows down, study the Word, and listen to anointed music and soak in His presence.

But King David replied to Araunah, "No, I insist on paying the full price. I will not take for the L<small>ORD</small> what is yours or sacrifice a burnt offering that costs me nothing."

So David paid Araunah six hundred shekels of gold for the site. David built an altar to the L<small>ORD</small> there and sacrificed burnt offerings and fellowship offerings. He called on the L<small>ORD</small>, and the L<small>ORD</small> answered him with fire from *heaven on the altar of burnt offering.* **1 Chronicles 21:24-25 (NIV)**

David not only had a heart for God, but he was a worshipper who was willing to pay the cost. Worshippers sacrifice praises, develop discipline, and dedicate time to be with the Lord. Later, you will find that there is a longing that you can't shake. Your time with the Lord becomes the air you breathe. If you miss spending time in worship and get caught up in the monotony of day to day routines, you may feel empty. Your Spirit demands and desires to be with the Lord. He is a good Father, and He's looking for true worshippers.

Yet a time is coming and has now come when the true worshipers will worship the Father in the Spirit and in truth, for they are the kind of worshipers the Father seeks. God is spirit, and his worshipers must worship in the Spirit and in truth." **John 4:23-24 (NIV)**

It's who you are and the way you live that count before God. Your worship must engage your spirit in the pursuit of truth. That's the kind of people the Father is out looking for: those who are simply and honestly themselves before him in their worship. God is sheer being itself—Spirit. Those who worship him must do it out of their very being, their spirits, their true selves, in adoration. **John 4:23-24 (MSG)**

A Heart for God

God is searching for those whose heart is towards Him. This love for our mighty God should be strong, and your desire should be to please and obey Him. Despite trials, tribulations, opposition, persecution, setbacks, and your desires, you should submit yourself to the Lord's will.

For the eyes of the LORD range throughout the earth to strengthen those whose hearts are fully committed to him. **2 Chronicles 16:9 (NIV)**

Once He sees your heart, He will prepare a heart check. During this checkup, He makes sure that it is functioning to its full compacity and has the right flow. Upon detection of any blockage, He will perform surgery and give you a blood transfusion.

Above all else, guard your heart, for everything you do flows from it. **Proverbs 4:23 (NIV)**

The blood of Jesus will heal you from your wounds so that you can release, forgive, surrender, and allow living waters to flow freely. It's not over. After this, you will receive a daily prescription of self-examination. The Holy Spirit will prompt you to search your heart for anything hindering you from being close to Him.

Search me, God, and know my heart; test me and know my anxious thoughts. **Psalm 139:23 (NIV)**

DANCING TO DESTINY

This agape love is not just for the Lord but for His people. The Lord will take you through a process to dismantle anything that's not like Him. He will build your character so that you will see like He sees and love as He loves. Your perspective will change, and you will quickly forgive and find grace and compassion for others. No longer will you judge and focus on the offense. Now you can see the hurt beyond the pain. Love is the key. You must operate in Love. It is through the greatest love of all that God gave His only Son for us. God is love.

Therefore, as God's chosen people, holy and dearly loved, clothe yourselves with compassion, kindness, humility, gentleness and patience. Bear with each other and forgive one another if any of you has a grievance against someone. Forgive as the Lord forgave you. And over all these virtues put on love, which binds them all together in perfect unity.

Let the peace of Christ rule in your hearts, since as members of one body you were called to peace. And be thankful. **Colossians 3:12-15 (NIV)**

Reflections: A Chosen People

When did God reveal that you were chosen to minister or to develop the ministry at church?

At what moment did you recognize the zeal and heart to dance?

How has the gift developed through you, and where do you see yourself now compared to when you first submitted to this ministry call?

2

The Purpose of Praise Dance

Wearing a linen ephod, David was dancing before the LORD with all his might
2 Samuel 6:14 (NIV)

The ultimate purpose of the praise dance ministry is to glorify God. The Lord is intentional and has multiple purposes through praise and worship. He uses ministers of praise dance to usher in the Holy Spirit so that the people are prepared for the Word to go forth.

Celebration

As we are praising the Lord, we can let go of our cares and focus on God. We remember who He is and all the great works He has done. Some would say, "He brought me from a mighty long way." Songs of celebration and high praise can assist you in helping to shake off anything that has kept you bound, as well as others. Don't let anyone or anything stop your praise.

Come, everyone! Clap your hands! Shout to God with joyful praise! For the LORD *Most High is awesome. He is the great King of all the earth.* **Psalm 47:1-2 (NIV)**

God has ascended with a mighty shout. The LORD *has ascended with trumpets blaring. Sing praises to God, sing praises; sing praises to our King, sing praises! For God is the King over all the earth. Praise him with a psalm. God reigns above the nations, sitting on his holy throne.* **Psalm 47:5-8**

When worshippers minister through songs of celebration, they are releasing hope, joy, strength, promises, declarations, and faith to the people. Soon after, those who are being encouraged will feel a sense of freedom and hope.

Warfare

Scripture says that there is a time and a season for everything under heaven (Ecclesiastes 3:1), including a time for war. The devil is real, and his demons are too! Oh yes, there are warlocks and witches. So, you might

DANCING TO DESTINY

want to stay away from Harry Potter. This movie tells about a young wizard who attends a school of witchcraft. Remember, what we see and hear affects our being. Our eyes and our ears are entry gates, which should be guarded at all times. There is no such thing as harmless entertainment; it all counts. Guard your gates!

Stay alert! Watch out for your great enemy, the devil. He prowls around like a roaring lion, looking for someone to devour. **1 Peter 5:8 (NLT)**

I will destroy the cities of your land and tear down all your strongholds.

I will destroy your witchcraft and you will no longer cast spells. **Micah 5:11-12 (NIV)**

We have been given authority in the powerful name of Jesus Christ. Merriam-Webster defines *authority* as power to influence or command thought, opinion, or behavior. Having authority means you are an authorized ambassador for Jesus. At the name of Jesus, everything must bow and submit. There is an immediate dispatch of warring angels to take charge and defeat the enemy. When you submit to God, and resist the devil, he shall flee (James 4:7).

That at the name of Jesus every knee should bow, in heaven and on earth and under the earth. **Philippians**

2:10 (NIV)

Years ago, when the Lord began to train me for my purpose, the first thing I began to encounter was warfare. I would frequently have dreams of battling with the enemy while I was in the praise dance ministry. In one of my dreams, dead bodies were running after me. It was an army. I was terrified and tried to find safety. Then I heard the Lord say, "You have the authority." I stopped immediately, turned around, and said, "I command you to bow to the name of Jesus." Suddenly, they all fell to their knees, and my fear was gone. I continued to tell them to worship the King. Wow! There's power in the name of Jesus! Use your authority.

Dance is your weapon. One day while spending intimate time with the Lord, I heard the Lord say, "You are my weapon." I wasn't sure about being a weapon, but I knew I heard the Lord. God speaks through His Word. So, I searched until I found the scripture to confirm His Word.

You are my war club, my weapon for battle— with you I shatter nations, with you I destroy kingdom. **Jeremiah 51:20 (NIV)**

God uses dance to defeat the enemy and to establish territories and regions. There is a triumphant sound. Can you hear it? We have the victory through Jesus. It was finished at the cross. In the end, we win!

Healing

God also uses the gift of dance for healing and deliverance. The ministry God created in me is for healing and breakthrough. I remember when I had a dream about being a part of the Houston Ballet. While in the dream, I was thinking to myself, "I don't fit here. They are professionals." Then I saw a lady who was sick, and I prayed for her. God healed the woman in the name of Jesus. God was revealing that healing would flow through the gift of dance.

For several years I experienced a lot of pain. In 2010, I was diagnosed with the chronic illness Crohn's, which was quite painful. I made several trips to the hospital and the emergency room throughout the year. This pain felt like I was going into labor. Up until this time, I was healthy and had never been sick. I even asked God if I was dying. The great news is God healed me supernaturally. I've been off the medicine for three years, and my last testing showed no signs of Crohn's (as stated by the Doctor). Without a special diet of any kind, the Lord healed me. I know it for myself. He is Rapha. Rapha means "to restore," "to heal," or "to make healthful" in Hebrew.

Later, I lost my marriage, my family, and my friends. I experienced betrayal and the loss of loved ones. These losses brought on emotional trauma, mental anguish, and heartache. I understand pain. However, your pain is a set up for your divine purpose.

The Spirit of the Sovereign LORD is on me because the LORD has anointed me to proclaim good news to the poor. He has sent me to bind up the brokenhearted, to proclaim freedom for the captives and release from darkness for the prisoners. **Isaiah 61:1 (NIV)**

When you come from out of the fire, you will come out as pure as gold. During this time, God was purifying me, building my character, and helping me to trust Him more.

Prophetic

God reveals the secret things to a prophet. Prophets are chosen vessels who speak and unfold the mysteries and the heart of God. Dance is a prophetic act, and prophetic acts demonstrate the word of God through flesh.

The Word became flesh and made his dwelling among us. We have seen his glory, the glory of the one and only Son, who came from the Father, full of grace and truth. **John 1:14 (NIV)**

Prophetic downloads come forth through dance as it

flows verbally. Prophetic dancers can move to recorded music or songs of the Lord. They are worshippers who spend a lot of time with God and dwell in His presence. Intimacy is imperative and breath to a prophet. They long to worship.

As praise dancers lead, people can see their expressions and full-body movement. They will SEE the message through dance by the leading of the Holy Spirit. Praise dance is a visual ministry. Some people are more visual, while others may be more audible. God is a creative God who has taken the art of dance to bring Him glory, honor, and praise.

Reflections: The Purpose of Praise Dance

How has the Lord revealed your purpose for praise dance?

Where do you think improvements can be made?

What next steps will you take?

3

The Tabernacle
God's Dwelling Place

The tabernacle was a tent, a sanctuary, or a place of worship. It was set up so that the people had a meeting place to worship God. God gave detailed instructions on what was to be built, how it was to be built, and how the people should approach God's dwelling place. The tabernacle is the protocol and the standard for worship, and that same standard remains today.

The Outer Court

There were three distinct areas in the tabernacle; the Outer Court, the Inner Court, and the Holy of Holies. The Outer Court was where they laid the offerings of animals for the atonement of sins. This place is where we forget about ourselves and focus on God. Here is where the priest washed their hands and feet. They purified and cleansed themselves to be acceptable and holy before God. There was a standard to come before God. Today we reflect, praise, forgive and repent in the outer court. This place can be a struggle sometimes because a shifting must take place as you press in.

The Inner Court

The Inner Court provided bread, continual lamp burning, and sweet incense in the **Holy of Holies,** which was separated by a curtain. This is the place that we pray, intercede for others, and are reminded of the sacrifice and the blood of Jesus. We give thanks, exalt and reverence God for who He is. Here is where we humble ourselves as we go before the throne. God is Sovereign. He is The Holy One; The Lion of Judah; Jehovah Jireh; The Great I Am; Alpha and Omega; The Beginning and the End. We press and press until there is a breaking and acceptance of our offering. The breaking is the shift that transitions you into the Holy of Holies.

The Holy of Holies

In the Holy Place was the Ark of the Covenant, which is symbolic of the promises to His people. Your covenant is your relationship with the Father. It is an agreement with God to submit as He's faithful to deliver on His promises.

This is how Aaron is to enter the Most Holy Place: He must first bring a young bull for a sin offering[a] and a ram for a burnt offering. ⁴ He is to put on the sacred linen tunic, with linen undergarments next to his body; he is to tie the linen sash around him and put on the linen turban. These are sacred garments; so, he must bathe himself with water before he puts them on. From the Israelite community he is to take two male goats for a sin offering and a ram for a burnt offering. "Aaron is to offer the bull for his own sin offering to make atonement for himself and his household. **Leviticus 16:3-7 (NIV)**

In the old testament, the priests were the only ones who had permission to go beyond the veil and stand before the mercy seat. They washed themselves and wore sacred garments of linen to go before God. The priests were to make an atonement for his sins and the sins of the people. Today, we are the priests! As priests, we come before God consecrated and purified as we prepare to go before His people. Now, we have access to go beyond the veil into the Holy of Holies. When Jesus died on the cross, the veil was torn. He offered Himself up for us. He is the Lamb of God and the ultimate sacrifice. He has paid the price and shed His blood so that we may be clean, healed, free, and delivered.

And when Jesus had cried out again in a loud voice, he gave up his spirit.

At that moment the curtain of the temple was torn in two from top to bottom. **Matthew 27:50-51 (NIV)**

Reflections: The Tabernacle: God's Dwelling Place

How does the Tabernacle relate to how you approach worship?

Where do you think improvements can be made?

What next steps will you take?

4

Our Offering To God

Obedience and Sacrifices

Jesus set a good example when he offered up His life so that we may live. Yes, He had reservations but ultimately submitted to the will of God. When you submit to His will, you have chosen to obey. Obedience is better than sacrifice (1 Samuel 15:22). Perhaps you will sacrifice your time, your praise, or your giving. A sacrifice is something you don't mind going the extra mile for, but obedience can place you in uncomfortable positions. My first thought, when the Lord is asking me to obey, is to run in the opposite direction.

On this journey of destiny, your obedience will be tested. God is looking for a permanent, "Yes." You must release your will in exchange for His. You must take up your cross and deny yourself.

Then he called the crowd to him along with his disciples and said: "Whoever wants to be my disciple must deny themselves and take up their cross and follow me. For whoever wants to save their life[will lose it, but whoever loses their life for me and for the gospel will save it. **Mark 8:34-35 (NIV)**

The Greek word for *deny* is APARNEOMAI. It means that a person must refuse to be thinking about oneself. It is a complete denial of your desires. Keep in mind, dying to self is a daily walk.

Sacrifices of Praise and Worship

There will be times when you don't feel like praising or worshipping, but this is a time to command your soul to praise the Lord. You must push past life's challenges and intense warfare. This testing will bring resilience and reliance upon the Lord. You will run into His presence and lift Him up because **Now** you know He really will keep you. You can continue to declare, "I'm not dead. I didn't lose my mind. I'm still standing etc." The secret place is where you will find safety. The secret place is your secret weapon!

He that dwelleth in the secret place of the most High shall abide under the shadow of the Almighty. **Psalm 91:1 (KJV)**

Offer Your Body as a Living Sacrifice

Your body is the temple of God. As a worshipper, you use your body as an offering and a weapon. As we partner with our lifestyles of holiness and consecration, the Glory of God can rest and flow through a willing vessel. Paul reveals to us in Romans that this is our reasonable worship.

Therefore, I urge you, brothers and sisters, in view of God's mercy, to offer your bodies as a living sacrifice, holy and pleasing to God—this is your true and proper worship. **Romans 12:1 (NIV)**

As obedient children, not fashioning yourselves according to the former lusts in your ignorance: But as he which hath called you is holy, so be ye holy in all manner of conversation; Because it is written, be ye holy; for I am holy. **1 Peter 1:14-16 (KJV)**

The struggle with lust is real. If you have a problem in this area, get you an accountability partner and read scriptures daily. Stay in the right environment and set boundaries. Develop a disciplined life of prayer, praise, and worship.

DANCING TO DESTINY

Being in a night club or having friends who enjoy frequent drinking may not be the environment or the support needed to remain consecrated and holy. You may wrestle in your flesh but get back up.

For I have the desire to do what is good, but I cannot carry it out. For I do not do the good I want to do, but the evil I do not want to do—this I keep on doing. Now if I do what I do not want to do, it is no longer I who do it, but it is sin living in me that does it. So, I find this law at work: Although I want to do good, evil is right there with me. For in my inner being I delight in God's law; but I see another law at work in me, waging war against the law of my mind and making me a prisoner of the law of sin at work within me. What a wretched man I am! Who will rescue me from this body that is subject to death? Thanks be to God, who delivers me through Jesus Christ our Lord! **Romans 7:19-25 (NIV)**

Now is an excellent time to receive healing and deliverance. Discern what you watch, hear or speak because your mind is a powerful tool. Wherever your mind goes, you will follow. Immediately switch to holy, good thoughts and begin to declare and decree scriptures that will shift your mind (Psalm 2:7). If you declare and decree a thing, it shall be established. There is a battle going on, so be determined to win even when the enemy lures you into temptation. Let the Spirit man lead you and walk in your freedom. There is power in the name of Jesus. He died for our sins so that we can live in freedom. He is our hope and our great deliver.

And they that are Christ's have crucified the flesh with the affections and lusts. If we live in the Spirit, let us also walk in the Spirit. **Galatians 5:24-25 (KJV)**

Legalism is helpless in bringing this about; it only gets in the way. Among those who belong to Christ, everything connected with getting our own way and mindlessly responding to what everyone else calls necessities is killed off for good—crucified. **Galatians 5:23-14 (MSG)**

DANCING TO DESTINY

Declarations for Holiness and Purity

- I have the mind of Christ (Romans 8:9)
- I have self-control
- I have set boundaries
- I can do all things through Christ who strengthens me (Philippians 4:13)
- I am more than a conquer through Christ (Romans 8:37)
- I die to my flesh so that I may live in Christ
- My life is holy and sanctified
- God is my strength and my rock (Psalm 18:2)
- I break the spirit of perversion and lust over my life in Jesus Name
- Every generation curse is broken in my life
- Let the fire of God consume my life and burn all impurities
- I am set free, healed, with nothing broken and nothing missing
- I break the spirit of loneliness in my life
- I am loved and complete in Christ. (Colossians 2:10)

Reflections: Our Offering to God

What are you offering to God, and how does it impact you when ministering?

Where do you think improvements can be made?

What next steps will you take?

5

Spiritual Preparation

Praying

According to Merriam-Webster, the definition of *prayer* is an address to God in word or thought: an earnest request: the act or practice of praying to God. Prayer is our communication with the Father. It is necessary to spend intimate time with God to hear, listen, and to receive. Pray for the message. Pray for the Vision. Pray for the ministry. This is the only way to know what God wants to deliver to His people for a divine moment. Your one on one time in the hidden place with God prepares you for your public moment to minister before His people, which is imperative. You can only carry what you have received in prayer and your time of worship with the King.

Intimacy with God is like getting to know someone new. The more time you spend with that person, the better you get to know them. You connect and gain more understanding of who they are and how they think. God is awesome and loving, and He has a sense of humor as well.

Knowledge of the Word

When I first joined the ministry of dance, my leader would pray the Word in prayer. I felt the power and saw it in action when she prayed. I was taught how important it was to know God's Word and be able to minister it through movement. You can't deliver a message without knowledge and understanding. Before ministers preach a sermon, they study the Word, listen, and pray. This is part of your preparation. You must study to show yourself approved.

Do your best to present yourself to God as one approved, a worker who does not need to be ashamed and who correctly handles the word of truth. **2 Timothy 2:15**

God deserves excellence. Every moment speaks because worshippers are the Word in flesh. Commit scriptures to memory one by one. The best way to start is to study the scriptures as they pertain to the message and commit them to memory.

Focus on the Message

Quiet your spirit. Remember, you are a priest. As a priest, before you go before God, consecrate yourself with fasting (use at your discretion) and praying. During your quiet time, listen to the song/message until you feel it in your Spirit. This will assist you to focus on the delivery to the people and should begin as soon as you start rehearsing until the message is delivered. You can do this at home, in your car, and of course, rehearsal.

Make use of your commute back and forth to work. Yes, this is an ongoing process. You will know once you have it in your spirit because every beat, sound, and words to the music will effortlessly flow with you. There will be no guessing or hesitation.

The song, as well as the movement, should become second nature before ministering. Remember that you should move to the song, and not lip sync as you minister. The focus should be on God and the delivery of the message to the people.

If you are a prophetic dancer, your preparation would be to quiet your spirit, pray, and fast. As God speaks the words of knowledge through your body, your spirit will move in sync with the Holy Spirit. The word of knowledge can be defined as the ability to know facts about a situation or a principle that is supernaturally revealed by the Lord. You may be thinking, "How can dance reveal words of knowledge"? Well, it's the same way God speaks through prophetic songs, art, and poems. He reveals Himself in the holy moment.

DANCING TO DESTINY

Reflections: Spiritual Preparation

How are you preparing for your Spiritual Preparation?

Where do you think improvements can be made?

What next steps will you take?

6

Outward Preparation
Garment Attire

Praise dancing is a visual ministry. If proper attire is not worn, the people could be distracted, and it can hinder the flow of the Holy Spirit. The flesh is weak. If the body becomes exposed inappropriately, you will lose the focus of the people and the delivery of the message. The devil will use any possible mishaps to garments to deviate the plan of God. Don't risk it. It's great to save money and cut overlays; however, if overlays risk any exposure of the flesh, don't use it. When in doubt, go without. Trust God to make provision for proper and holy garment attire!

Garments should never be worn after the message has

gone forth unless the dance ministry sits together as a body. Once you finish ministering, go to a quiet room to pray out as a ministry. Pray and thank God for all He has done through you. Then remove your garments to change into standard attire. You can wear a covering to pull over your garment if you decide to walk around.

Let all things be done decently and in order. **1 Corinthians 14:40 (KJV)**

Overlays

Overlays or t-shirts (may be appropriate at times) should extend beyond the buttocks. Garments should be loose fitting with no images of silhouettes. Again, remember the flesh is weak. If a silhouette is shown, someone can become focused on the shape of a person and miss the message. Keep in mind; there are struggles with the flesh. Avoid anything form-fitting that may trigger ungodly memories, which may distract from the demonstration of God. In addition, make sure that you are adequately covered for rehearsals.

Undergarments

Undergarments should always be double layered. A long sleeve unitard bodysuit can be worn with an overlay and palazzo pants. You can also wear a dress over the unitard; however, palazzo pants or culottes should be worn underneath. If you use a leotard, tights should be worn (preferably the same color); then the top layers (overlay and palazzo pants). When choosing a unitard or a leotard, avoid "v" scoop necks. A high neck or a crew neck is preferred for full coverage.

Preferred underwear and bras should be solid black. Avoid prints, flowers, special designs, etc. I recommend you carry an extra set of underwear in your garment bag. If you sweat a lot during the message, you can change and freshen up.

Shoes

The praise dance team may choose to dance with shoes or without. Avoid wearing flip flops while in your garments. Remember, presentation is critical, and God deserves excellence.

Jewelry

Jewelry should not be worn while you minister unless it is your wedding rings. You should avoid wearing earrings as this can be a risk for any dancer. Keep in mind the ministry should look like one body.

DANCING TO DESTINY

Fingernail Polish

Fingernail polish is beautiful, but can also become a distraction. Some ministries allow French manicures to stay unified while others prefer no polish. Use your discretion, and remember it's not about us. The focus is on Jesus and giving God the glory.

Hair Styles

Finally, the hair. Yes. Hair can also be a distraction. The preferred way is to push back and pull up. You can choose to wear a high bun, side bun, or low bun. Dancers are known to wear buns for balance and to focus on the art of dance. Ponytails or braids can also be worn with discretion (hip hop or warfare) but pulled away from the face. Free-flowing hairstyles can be beautiful, but distracting from the message. If the minister of dance becomes a character in the message (portraying a person in the song or a play), wearing a free-flowing hairstyle may be appropriate, which can help to bring the Word of God to life. Pray and make sure it is Spirit-led.

Reflections: Outward Preparation

How are you preparing for your Outward Preparation?

Where do you think improvements can be made?

What next steps will you take?

7

Choreography & Pageantry
Choreography

Choreograph is defined by Merriam-Webster as the composition and arrangement of dances. It is the art of symbolically representing dancing. Ministers of dance should keep all movements holy. Of course, the most creative choreographer is the Lord. He gives vision and divine downloads. It's also important to study the art of dance for excellence. If you don't have any dance experience taking classes will give you more confidence to minister. I didn't have experience with dancing, so occasionally, I would take a class at a local studio. I would also practice at home and spend time learning and perfecting movements for messages. It is important to give God your all so that He is honored. Always give God your best!

As ministers of dance, movements should remain holy and acceptable unto God. Since this is ministry, it will take on a life of its own. It is God's Word, message, or warfare brought forth through movement.

Prophetic Dance

Ministers of dance can also be prophetic or hold the office of the Prophet. Some prophets receive words of knowledge from God with direct downloads during worship. A powerful demonstration of God's Spirit can be seen with ministers of dance moving with a song of the Lord. In conjunction with prophetic psalmists, songs of the Lord (prophetic worship music) can be released during this time as well.

Then Miriam the prophet, Aaron's sister, took a timbrel in her hand, and all the women followed her, with timbrels and dancing. **Exodus 15:20 (NIV)**

Some refer to prophetic dance as moving in the spirit. As you grow and mature as ministers, you can learn to move with the flow of worship, otherwise known as improvisation. *Improvisation* means flowing, creating, or inventing movement. This skill set can be taught and requires focus on God and the message; and not on steps or movement only. So, hear the sound of the music, dance to the beat and flow in the Holy Spirit.

Pageantry

Pageantry is an extravagant display or ceremony in which props are used for worship. The splendor of God's glory can be displayed through pageantry. It creates a glorious processional for praise and worship while ministering.

Here are a few props many worshippers used:

- Flags

- Banners

- Crowns

- Billows

- Scepter

- Staff

Jehovah Nissi is the Lord our **Banner**. He is our Victory. It is symbolic that every battle has already been won. It is a declaration of possessing the land the Lord has given to us.

And Moses built an altar and called its name, The-Lord-Is-My-Banner; for he said, "Because the Lord has sworn: the Lord will have war with Amalek from generation to generation. **Exodus 17:15-16 (NKJV)**

DANCING TO DESTINY

Reflections: Choreography and Pageantry

How has your Choreography developed for ministry?

Where do you think improvements can be made?

What next steps will you take?

8

Leadership

Servant Leadership

Great leaders are servants who have been promoted. If you humble yourself, He will lift you up (James 4:10 NIV). Some leaders are born, and others are built. The possibilities are endless. The key is to study and continue to grow. Leaders should lead by example and operate with a spirit of excellence. What you establish as a leader will set the expectations for the ministers of dance. If the ministry teaches timeliness and commitment, this will be the expectation and the response.

Let all things be done decently and in order. **1 Corinthians 14:40 (KJV)**

Leaders should operate in and teach others how to love. Sooner or later, someone may be offended, but you must be quick to forgive and love others on the journey.

Prayer, warfare, and scripture should be taught. We are to operate in our authority through the name of Jesus. Our primary responsibility is to lead others to Jesus Christ, our Lord, and Savior. We are the light, and God is the source who gives light. Without the source, there's darkness. So stay plugged into the source and let the light shine for the Glory of God.

Lastly, leaders should develop other leaders and leave a legacy. You should be able to duplicate your God-given gifts so that others can go out and reproduce; which is the fruit of your labor.

And he said to them, "Go into all the world and proclaim the gospel to the whole creation. **Mark 16:15 (ESV)**

Reflections: Leadership

How has leadership impacted your ministry?

Where do you think improvements can be made?

What next steps will you take?

DANCING TO DESTINY

www.ingramcontent.com/pod-product-compliance
Lightning Source LLC
Chambersburg PA
CBHW070209100426
42743CB00013B/3118